A bull elephant in Kruger National Park.

A Memory of Elephants

On Safari in South Africa

Harriet Saunders

Copyright © 2014 Harriet Saunders

All rights reserved. No part of this publication may be reproduced in any form or by any means without prior written permission of the author and publisher.

ISBN-13: 978-0-692-24355-8

ISBN-10: 0-692-24355-0

Chalouise Books
P.O. Box 1835
Rohnert Park, CA 94928

ChalouiseBooks@comcast.net

Disclaimer, apology and dedication

It is possible that, despite my very best efforts, I have misidentified a few of the animals. The elephants in particular are hard to tell apart on short acquaintance. I know I have misheard, misunderstood, or misspelled many names of both people and places. I suspect I have also misremembered events here and there even with the photographic evidence as a guide. I have tried to be accurate, though I must admit, not at the expense of the narrative. It turns out I am a storyteller, not a journalist. So please forgive my liberties and my mistakes and enjoy the story.

I would like to dedicate this book to all the animals who enormously enrich our lives while we humans steadily diminish theirs. They need our help, even if it is just spending tourist dollars in Africa. Please do what you can.

Foreword

> A journey of a thousand miles begins beneath your feet.
>
> —Lao Tzu, *Tao Te Ching*, verse 64

> A crash of rhinos, a bloat of hippopotamuses, an implausibility of gnus, an obstinacy of buffalo, a journey of giraffes, a dazzle of zebras, a memory of elephants...
>
> —terms found in *An Exaltation of Larks*, by James Lipton

I was nine when *Born Free* was published. I devoured all three books about Elsa as they became available and daydreamed about keeping a lion. I read Gerald Durrell's *Rosy is my Relative* and daydreamed about keeping an elephant. I read the rest of his books and daydreamed of adventures with animals in the wilderness.

Last December, through sheer happenstance, I listened to an audiobook by Lawrence Anthony called *The Elephant Whisperer*. I was entranced by the story of the rogue herd of elephants rescued by the compassion and determination of the author. Because I was listening rather than holding the actual book, I had no idea that Thula Thula, the game reserve in the book, was a real place. I didn't even know how to spell it. However, a few minutes spent poking around on the internet led to the discovery not only of the right way to spell the name but also that the luxury lodge mentioned in the book had come to fruition and was actually affordable.

I started daydreaming about what my ideal African trip would look like. I tried hard to get my husband Robert interested in the idea, but he adamantly did not want to go. I thought about what I would need to do to make it possible to go by myself. I looked at packaged safari tours (the internet is a wonderful place) and rapidly realized that not only could I not afford what was on offer, I also didn't like the idea of spending so little time in each place. It takes me awhile to learn my way around, to learn people's names, to have a sense of place. So I started exploring the idea of staying for 10 days at Thula Thula, with some day trips to nearby national parks. I found cheap airline tickets and figured out connections. I found a budget tour company called Outlook Safari with a hotel in Johannesburg so I could deal safely with jet lag, add 5 days in Kruger National Park and get to see a little more of the country. I studied maps and looked everything up on Google Earth. I figured out transportation to and from the Johannesburg and Durban airports so I wouldn't have to drive. In short, I planned a very nice trip, but nothing I said would induce Robert to join me and I hesitated to commit to it.

One evening in early March, the movie *Up* was shown on TV. Robert and I pretty much never watch movies on TV, but for some reason, Robert wanted to watch this one. I made a bowl of popcorn and we sat at the kitchen table watching on the little kitchen TV. (Why on earth we didn't go into the living room and watch on the big TV, I have no idea. We like the kitchen best, I guess.) It was a wonderful movie about a girl determined to have an adventure and the boy who promises her one. They grow up, get married, have a happy, busy life together, but the adventure keeps getting postponed. And then she dies. The movie is mostly about the man when he is old and has to live with that huge regret. As soon as the movie finished, I went upstairs and booked my adventure.

About a month later, a friend of Robert's told him to quit talking about it, grab the opportunity and just go already, so he decided to go. It was not easy but I managed to book him into everything. I even managed to get seat assignments together on our flights.

I spent the next four months preparing: reading, making lists, trying out equipment, breaking in hiking boots, finding the exact right hat. I took a seminar on wildlife photography. I downloaded field guides and the CDC's Yellow Book (full of dread diseases you really don't want to know about) onto my iPad. And then spent a week with a fever after getting all the inoculations to avoid those dread diseases. It took me weeks to pack—and I was glad to have spent the time as there were essential things I would have forgotten. Robert did buy a hat and boots and spent about an hour packing the day we left.

On September 24th at 6:00 p.m., my daughter Brook drove us to meet the airport shuttle. I had butterflies in my stomach and could hardly believe that the time had finally come. Robert quoted Lao Tzu as we walked out the door.

Chapter 1

September 26th

The flight out is as bad as I expected it to be. Addis Abba is a nightmare of confusion, exhaustion and an almost complete lack of services. Ethiopian Airlines bought several Boeing Dreamliners, but I guess they spent all their money on the planes because their airport is not equipped to handle that many passengers at once. There is no jet way, so we bump our luggage down a long, long stairway, take a bus across the tarmac and then schlep our luggage up a long, long stairway. I am only able to do this because other passengers help me. In the airport the gates are insanely crowded, there is no gate or flight information available, there is no food available, and there is one women's bathroom with three stalls and no toilet paper. Robert walks the whole length of the terminal before he finds out which gate we need. It is the same as where we deplaned. When it is time to board, we bump our luggage down a long, long stairway, take a bus across the tarmac, schlep our luggage up a long, long stairway and we are back in the same plane where we started.

We are not met at the Johannesburg airport as expected and I think I am too tired to cope. But I am armed with a cell phone and phone numbers and the problem is eventually solved. We are driven to our hotel by a young taciturn fellow wearing blue jeans and a flawlessly ironed oxford shirt.

I am so tired I can hardly function beyond taking an absolutely essential shower. I sleep solidly for 4 hours before dinner. Dinner is tasty, but I'm too tired to eat much and am back in bed by 8:00 p.m. local time.

Right: *The Outlook Safari Lodge is an oasis of calm and beauty in the blare and glare of Johannesburg.*

September 27th

Today is our first full day in Africa. We are driving from Johannesburg to Kruger National Park. Riding with us is another Outlook guest. I'm not sure we were introduced. I don't know his name. It takes about 5 hours and seems very long—somehow longer than the 30 hour plane ride when I wasn't expecting anything to happen and it didn't. Now I am eager for action but instead am looking at an endless unprepossessing countryside. It looks a little like Oakdale—rolling hills with small trees—except that it goes on and on and I can't identify any of the trees. There are also a lot of scruffy industrial buildings, warehouses and factories. I see two cooling towers from a power plant, well away from the main road and looming eerily in the smog. We pass several trains filled with coal. A.D., our driver/guide, says that coal is the country's main source of electricity. The air pollution is bad, an unlovely brown mix of dust and coal smoke.

Air quality improves as we get further away from the city. We stop for lunch at a big truck and tourist stop. There are ostriches out back. The doors on the stalls in the bathroom go all the way from the floor to the ceiling. This turns out to be a common feature throughout our trip. A little claustrophobic, but nice and private. I have a hard time figuring out something I can eat amongst the fast food offerings and end up with a soggy grilled cheese sandwich and warm orange juice.

We continue on our journey and pass acres and acres of trees planted for harvesting. The green is refreshing, though the ugly patches where the trees have recently been cut aren't. We pass a citrus orchard and a huge banana farm.

Once in the park (finally!) we start seeing animals right away. The first one is a buffalo. I don't know if it is a Cape buffalo or even if there are different types. (It turns out that it is and there aren't.) The buffalo is grazing along the river and too far away to see properly. Then there are zebras. Next, we see impala. A.D. tells us not to get too excited about them. There are approximately a gazillion impala in the park. But at least they all look well fed and healthy.

Left: *The first warthog sighting—running away with her silly tail stuck straight up behind her.*

Opposite: *An encounter with an angry elephant. Yikes!*

There are a couple of elephants obscured by the brush, so I can't see them well at all. A little further down the road there are a few more. Then we discover one all alone. I'm assuming he is a bull. I stick my camera out the van window to get a picture and really piss him off. He erupts onto the road and comes at us in a rush. A.D. calmly backs the van away and mildly remarks, "You know these guys can be dangerous, right?" The elephant, once he sees we are retreating, gives his head a disgusted and disdainful toss and continues across the road. His scorn could not be more clearly expressed: "#$%! tourists."

We arrive in camp mid-afternoon and are offered a welcoming (and much appreciated) cold drink and then we are driven to our tent.

It is 105° outside the tent and more inside. I put my insulin in the little refrigerator for safe keeping.

As part of our Outlook itinerary, we get to go on a SANParks (South African National Parks) night drive. The park

guides are the only ones allowed to stay out past the gate curfew of 6 p.m. (I love the fact that here the humans are confined while the animals are free to roam.) Unfortunately our driver seems to be in an big hurry. We see a family of elephants I would love to spend time with—he pauses for 5 minutes max. We see elephants by the river. He pauses not at all. We drive out on a bridge over the Sabi River. The scenery is breathtakingly beautiful. It is, of course, green along the river. The sun is setting bright red, the water flows silver over sandstone rocks. There are baboons on the shore, hippos in the water and a kingfisher hunting from a rock. All this merits two minutes of his time.

On our way to the river, we spotted a dead impala that had been hoisted into a tree by a leopard, though there was no leopard to be seen. We come back after it gets dark and using spotlights, manage to actually see a mama leopard with her cub. Sort of. The thicket was extremely thickety and the cats are visible only when they move and even then only intermittently. I can't get a decent picture. We spend an inordinate amount of time peering fruitlessly through the brambles. Really, *Animal Planet* does leopards much better.

Above right: *Robert ala Teddy Roosevelt.*
Above: *The Sabi River at sunset.*

The one thing we are actually allowed time to enjoy is a pride of lionesses complete with mamas, aunties, and cubs of varying ages. They make cat noises and roll all over the grass and each other. The cubs swagger around like tough guys until they fall over their own feet. They then get up and trot off nonchalantly as though that is what they planned all along. One mama makes the milk bar available right near us. We watch while the cubs gorge themselves and then snuggle afterward for a bit of a wash and brush up from mom. All of this is illuminated by the big hand-held spotlights. I'm not sure who is holding them. I only know they aren't holding them still, making photography problematic at best.

And then (sigh) we drive around a lot in the dark going too fast to see anything. Except we do see a honey badger, which is definitely cool.

ABOVE AND RIGHT: *Lion cubs of various ages.*
BELOW: *Yum!*

Above: *Mama and baby.*

Left: *A honey badger moseying alongside the road.*

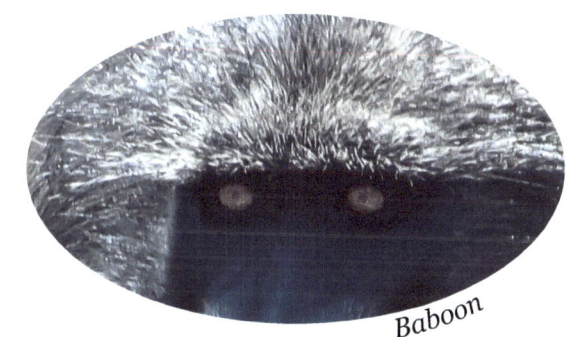
Baboon

Chapter 2

September 28th

The smell of smoke wakes me up in the middle of disorienting darkness. I am alarmed, but finally figure out that it is coming from the controlled burns we saw yesterday outside the camp. The fear of fire while sleeping in a bone dry canvas tent situated right next to bone dry grass and trees is no small thing. It takes me a long time to go back to sleep. I am awake again at 5 a.m.—I estimate I got about 2 hours of sleep—but this time I have to roll out of bed as we need to be at the main Outlook tent by 5:30 for the morning game drive.

I emerge from the tent into a sweet, inviting morning and no longer regret having to wake up so early. It cooled down overnight. There are puffy pink clouds and the light is soft and gentle. The birds are already up and about, making cheerful noise. I have absolutely no clue as to their identity. I can hear them but I can't see them.

Tea, fruit and rusks are served before we leave on our drive. Up until now I had no idea what a rusk was—now I know. It is a poor imitation of a biscotti, chunky and tough, too thick to dunk to soften, too hard to actually eat. I have a pear. So far, I haven't had enough to eat at a single meal on this trip.

RIGHT: *(from left to right) Debbie, me, and Robert.*

For this morning's drive we go with the manager of the Outlook camp, Debbie. She is young, short and stocky, a blond, sunburned, rough edged South African with a thick Afrikaans accent. (The Afrikaans accent sounds like an overdone exaggeration of an Australian accent by an actor with a tin ear—it is a little hard to understand.) She does not wear the stresses of her job well.

Again we see elephants right away, three of them, mother, baby and teenager, tearing up some bushes. Literally tearing them apart, making the thicket a little less thickety. (There are conservationist who claim that this is exactly what the trouble with elephants is, this destroying of habitat. They are probably correct, but just right now I don't agree.) The sun is barely up and the elephants are beautiful in the gold light. They are aware of us but continue to peacefully, albeit noisily, consume their breakfast. And again, we do not spend enough time, but at least it is more than yesterday.

ABOVE: *Mama works her way methodically through twigs, grass and leaves.*

RIGHT: *Her adolescent offspring shows off his tree stripping skills with gusto.*

And then we are back to the endless leopard hunt. There is one very young Aussie girl on our truck who is so excited about the whole thing that it is hard to begrudge her the time. I do get one really good look at the cat leaping through the underbrush, but unfortunately, not a good picture.

We see many birds along the way. We don't have to actually go looking for birds. They are everywhere and plentiful.

Above: *Southern yellow-billed hornbill*
Above right: *Hooded vulture*
Right: *Wahlberg's eagle*

We see a large troop of baboons and spend some time watching them. There are all ages, including a couple of big males I would not like to meet in a dark alley. They have big teeth and they look fierce. They are opportunistic omnivores, which I didn't know until today. Mostly they eat grass and seeds and small amounts of insects and small animals.

Above: *A baby baboon suckles while his mom grooms him.*

Left: *A crocodile on the sandbank.*

Right: *A baboon poses for tourists on the river bridge.*

The first botanical identification is a wild cucumber twining up a thorn tree.

One person asks if it is a parasite, but Debbie says no, though she can't remember the term for neither parasitic nor symbiotic. I know I know this word and after five minutes of really working at it, I finally manage to pull it out of my brain: commensal. I hope I got it right. (I did look it up later and I did get it right. Yay me.)

Other sightings:

- A big mama warthog with wicked looking tusks

ABOVE: *Wild cucumber*

LEFT: *Mama warthog and her almost full grown baby.*

BELOW: *Oxpecker birds help keep animals free of ticks and flies.*

- Oxpecker birds on an impala

- Banded mongooses (Ah, the eternal question: shouldn't it be mongeese? But the dictionary says no.)

- And the occasional giraffe looming over the proceedings with goofy aloofness.

Above: *We see this banded mongoose in camp.*

Left: *There are 9 subspecies of giraffes. All the ones we see are* Giraffa camelopardalis giraffa, *the South African or Cape giraffe.*

We get back to the dining area about 9 a.m. I must say, this is definitely a young person's gig here. The schedule does not take into account the extra bathroom breaks and sleep needed by us old folks. The youngsters evidently think nothing of sitting down to breakfast without a bathroom break. I do not appreciate this. Which reminds me to mention that the ablutionary facilities are woefully inadequate—not sure what we will do about this. Robert hasn't even been able to shave, there being no outlets available in the men's bathroom. We are both looking pretty scrudzy. I devoutly hope there are more creature comforts available at Thula Thula. I know, I know. I needed low budget for this portion of the trip to be able to afford it at all. So I guess I'm getting what I paid for and I should stop complaining.

RIGHT: *The Outlook camp. Debbie is preparing her truck for the next game drive. Another guide waits in front of the kitchen tent with welcoming drinks for incoming guests. The dining area is toward the back.*

LEFT: *Surprise! I meet this warthog face to face at the bathroom door. He is kind enough to wait for me to fetch my camera. We hang out together for a lovely piggy half hour, before I had to leave for the evening drive.*

The evening drive starts with what Outlook calls a snack, but we call lunch. There is cheese and crackers, fruit, cookies. Stuff I can eat! But my tummy is upset, so I don't eat much.

There is a newcomer on the truck and I note that Debbie has a sharp word for her, just as she did for us when we first got here. But she is very nice to us now and I am enjoying her company. She is passionate about the animals, talented at finding them and both incredibly knowledgeable and willing to share her knowledge about the area's natural history, ecology, and conservation efforts.

I ask her who picks up the litter. There isn't a lot of it and it is mostly just along the road by the camp entrance, but it is jarring. It seems like we should just stop and pick up what we see. Debbie says that is not a good idea because it is very dangerous to get out of the truck. She says the guides draw straws for the "chicken patrol" picking up garbage and getting back into the safety of the truck just as fast as they can.

For the first part of the drive we go to an area of rocky outcroppings. The trees are different—there are more ficus trees, fewer and bigger acacias and much less of the thorny underbrush. Debbie says the animals are different too, and sure enough, we spot two antelope not found anywhere else.

Right: *The klipspringers' hooves are adapted to walking on rocks and they never set foot on the ground. They are relatively easy to spot.*

Left: *The steenbok is small, shy and hard to see, but Debbie is looking for it, and so we get lucky.*

Opposite: *A rocky outcropping in Kruger National Park.*

Further along, we stop in the middle of the road to admire a kudu browsing on a tree and then notice three lionesses setting up for a kill. Debbie quietly polls her guests to make sure none of us will freak out if the kill actually happens, but we are all eager to watch the excitement. Lioness 1 is along the road a little ahead of us, Lioness 2 is in the grass a ways off the road to the left of the kudu, and Lioness 3 is stealthily making her way around to the other side of the kudu, to drive him towards the other two.

Above: *Lioness 2 waits for her sisters to get into position.*
Opposite top: *The kudu barks.*
Opposite bottom: *The scary stare of lioness 1.*

The kudu catches the scent of them and gives a sharp loud warning bark. Lioness 1 rushes toward him before Lioness 3 is in place. In a flash the kudu is gone, leaping across the road behind the truck and disappearing into the bush.

Lioness 1 walks right up to the truck with the quintessential cat look of "Yeah, that was exactly what I meant to do." She sits there for a while looking at us and we sit very, very still. There is nothing at all between her and us and we are trying very hard to not look like prey. It is spine-chilling to be stared at by a lion. Then she plops down in the road right in front of the truck, yawns and washes her face. She is joined briefly by Lioness 2 and then all three of them wander across the road to goof off in the shade. They must not have been very hungry.

Left: *Lioness 1 in the road.*
Below: *Those teeth!*
Bottom: *Nice kitty.*

Opposite top: *Lionesses relaxing.*
Opposite middle: *Now you see the cubs...*
Opposite bottom: *...and now you don't.*

Then we spot their cubs. There are five of them walking parallel to the road but about five feet into the bush. We follow along coasting quietly in the truck. They are making their way to what Debbie says is a predetermined hiding place, chosen by their moms to keep them safe while the moms hunt. But the cubs are playing around, in no hurry to do what they should. Even moving and playing and making no effort to hide they are difficult to see in the dense thicket.

When they finally settle down, they are almost impossible to see. I can just make out one set of ears and that only because I know the cubs are there.

We continue driving when it becomes obvious that the cubs are not going to stir from their hiding place and the lionesses have gone to sleep under their tree. We see many birds and other creatures, but the most significant event is that one of the young people announces that he has to go pee. This is a serious problem. There are only a few places where it is safe to get out of the truck, none of them nearby. It is almost time to head back to camp and if Debbie drives to one of the safe spots, she will almost certainly miss the curfew. On the other hand, if he really really has to go NOW, then a safe spot would be closer than camp. In the end, the young man makes it back to camp and Debbie makes sure there is time for bathroom breaks before and after all the rest of the drives. I am very grateful for that young man's courage in speaking up.

There are eleven of us at dinner and we are an eclectic, cosmopolitan group. There is a Jewish lady from Florida, who I nickname Chatty Cathy, because she is. There is a couple from New Zealand. I never hear their names, but really enjoy their conversation. There is the man who rode out from Johannesburg with us, a middle aged Finnish chap I will call Henrik. It might even actually be his name. He is a big man with a big square head, probably in his mid to late 40s, dressed in the chinos, untucked white t-shirt and scuffed blue tennies of a teenager circa 1970. There is a delightful young Frenchman from London, named Gilliam, a mother and son from Israel (he's the one who broke the bathroom deadlock), a middle-aged, beautiful blonde from Denmark and a sweet, shy boy from Brazil.

The dinner is laid out on one long table under a canvas canopy, lit by hanging lanterns and candles on the table. The lighting is just barely adequate, but lovely. The conversation, helped along by liberal servings of wine, is far ranging and fun. Gilliam describes shark cage diving in Cape Town. I ask him lots of questions as it sounds scary and interesting at the same time. I've heard about it and want details. We all discuss the Yosemite fire at great length. The non-Americans know as much or more about it than we do. For some reason, American football head injuries comes up as a topic—I have no idea why. We talk about dairy farming in New Zealand, growing horse hay in Finland, vineyards in Cape Town, and today's soccer match between New Zealand and South Africa. (South Africa won. That is all I glean from the immense amount of information being bandied about.) It is a most congenial meal.

Debbie talks to me during dinner about going on a bush walk tomorrow morning. I really want to do it, but, like the night drive, it is run by SANParks and will be open to others besides Outlook guests. She is concerned that I won't be able to keep up. I concede her point, graciously I hope, but I am disappointed. I will go on the usual morning drive instead.

The Outlook camp.

Chapter 3

September 29th

It is cold and has started raining, making for a wet and uncomfortable morning drive. Not many animals are out and about (smart animals). Debbie has provided us with hot water bottles and fleece-lined ponchos, which help some, but I am miserable by the time we get back to camp.

The animal list for this morning is short: Kudu; impala; a mama rhino with an older baby; wildebeests locking horns but without any real heat; many giraffes including two butting heads, also rather laconically; two elephants too far away to really see; a few birds. I'm having a hard time hearing Debbie when she identifies them. I'm wearing over my ears my sweatshirt hood, my rain jacket hood and the fleece-lined hood of the poncho. I can't imagine why I can't hear. She is more than a little impatient when asked to repeat herself. I'm glad I sprang for the good bird book. I have rain gear for my camera, but am too uncomfortable to take many pictures. Robert went on the bush walk. He saw the same rhinos we did and nothing else.

Before breakfast, I mention to Debbie that my stomach is really upset. She opines, and several other people agree with her, that it is the Malarone anti-malarial pills that are probably making me sick. Since I haven't seen a single mosquito in Kruger and Thula Thula is in a malaria free area, stopping them is a no-brainer. So nice to have that problem solved. I'm sure it will take a while to wear off. I don't feel good and breakfast still looks inedible, but at least there's hope.

Another Londoner has joined the group. Andy is a tall, thin and personable young man who plunges into the general conversation with relish. Chatty Cathy is in fine form this morning. She decides to lecture the Israeli woman from Jerusalem on how to keep a kosher kitchen. She has it all wrong and the Israeli lets her know in no uncertain terms. Her solicitude towards me because I am not feeling well is officious, cloying and really irritating. As contrasted with the two young men from London who are both concerned and attentive, but seem to understand that I want to ignore the whole situation. Andy expresses concern that my "I'm fine" to Chatty Cathy is so breathy. Then Robert asks me how I am doing and I answer with more than a little asperity, "I'm fine". I turn to Andy and ask if that is better and everyone laughs and leaves me alone. Except Chatty Cathy. Fortunately, the conversation becomes more general, and much more interesting. Gilliam talks about how much he dislikes the arrogance of the French even though he is a French citizen and lives in London because he can't stand Paris. He and Andy compare notes on the London scene and find places and people in common.

There is a discussion of the relative merits of New York and London and we move on from there to mountain climbing. I'm enjoying these free-wheeling conversations.

After breakfast, Robert and I walk over to the store. There is a winding path along the river, paved with concrete and bricks with a decorative log fence inside an ugly but highly functional electrified elephant fence. We walk a little ways on it. I see a few birds but not the elephants, hippos and crocs I am hoping for. It feels so good to be setting my own animal watching pace that I could stay out here for hours. Unfortunately, Robert is bored and I have no clue how to get back to our tent on my own, so I can't stay. We buy a map and laundry soap at the store. I am looking for souvenirs but the selection is hopeless. I buy a few postcards. Then, as we walk back to our tent, I pay close attention to our route. Tomorrow I will follow the river path to my heart's content.

Above Right: *The fence along the river.*
Middle: *The Sabi river near camp.*
Right: *Red-billed spurfowl*

On the way back to our tent, I hear a bird whose call sounds exactly like "tweet, tweet". I can't see him, of course, so I can't identify him. Other birds, like this spurfowl, make no noise, but are easy to see.

Highlights from the evening drive:

- ❖ More birds, lots and lots of birds.

Top: *Marabou storks*
Top right: *Egyptian goose*
Above: *African grey hornbill*
Right: *Hamerkop*

- Hooded vultures feasting on a very whiffy giraffe carcass. I know they hold a valuable place in the ecosystem as the cleanup crew, but eww.

- A hyena walking with determination down the road. We go in front of her and turn so we can see her face. She immediately veers off the road into the bush and continues trotting parallel to the road until she is in front of us again. At which point she cuts back onto the road and proceeds on her way. A hyena on a mission.

- A large herd of Cape buffalo, at least 30 animals, which we sit in the middle of for a while. Mostly they ignore us, though four of the really big guys stare daggers at us until they get bored and forget.

- Hippos in the river, about 14 of them. The adults imitate rocks in the middle of the water and are hard to see, though they do show themselves now and then.

❖ Some young hippos are playing in the water—such fun to watch. (At least I assume they are playing, though the teeth don't look too playful.)

❖ A mama hippo is foraging on the river bank with her baby. Another one calls to her and soon there is a concert of hippos yodeling. The light is almost gone, so no more pictures, but it is the grunts and roars that are particularly entertaining anyway.

Chapter 4

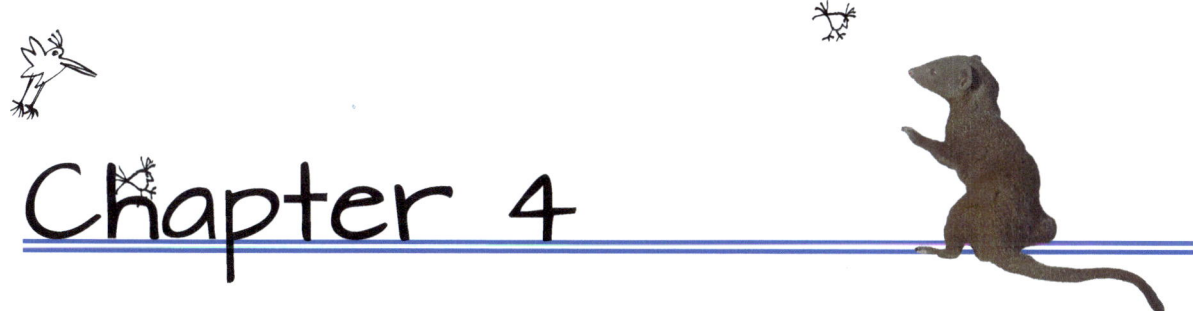

September 30th

It's 4:15 a.m. I'm trying to write on my iPad, but it is cumbersome and slow, and I can't stay awake. There is no place in our tent to set up the laptop, making it very difficult to get any work done. On the other hand, I can't seem to stay asleep for more than an hour or two at a time. It is probably not a coincidence that that is approximately the interval between Robert's trips to the bathroom.

Henrik, our Finnish friend, went home yesterday. He was on his way to Cape Town for an egg convention, as he is a sales representative for an egg company. It took me forever to understand "egg" with his accent. He told us many stories and jokes. I wish I could remember them all—he was very funny—but here are the only two I've managed to retain.

On a trip to Russia, when it was still the USSR, he quickly became aware of the paucity of goods available in the grocery stores. One day he noticed bananas for sale and commented about it to his guide. The guide's response was, "The monkeys in the zoo must be on vacation." He tells this story after I ask if there are any more bananas left in the fruit bowl. (There aren't.)

The second story was injected into a discussion of driving on the right vs. the left side of the road. He prefaced it by saying that all Scandinavian countries tell jokes about each other and it is all meant in good fun. So. We all know that Sweden is a democracy. It is a very democratic country, always making decisions democratically. When they were trying to determine if they should switch from driving on the left to driving on the right, they put it to a vote. The results were split exactly even, so they decided to switch the private vehicles the first year and the commercial vehicles the second.

It is still raining when we walk to the dining tent before the morning drive. Yesterday was so cold and uncomfortable, I am not looking forward to today. The poncho and hot water bottle are doing little to keep me warm. Thoughts of hot chocolate keep creeping in.

With little to see in the way of animals, I talk to Debbie. She has gotten friendlier over time and I learn a little more about her. She is from the Limpopo province and grew up on a farm. She has been guiding for 5 years, though only 8 months in Kruger. She defines herself as a wildlife artist, working mainly with pencil drawing. She takes reference photos while driving tourists about and figures, for her, this is an ideal job.

We have a long discussion about elephant culling. She is in favor because the elephant population has outgrown the space available and the elephants are destroying habitat essential for the survival of other species. When giraffes browse on a tree to the point of stress, the tree produces tannins which the giraffes don't like. The tree also gives off a pheromone that warns nearby trees to do the same, so the giraffes have to move some distance away to find edible food. The elephants don't care. They just eat whatever they want whenever they want it and ingest a lot of tannin. Debbie feels the culling is humane because rangers skilled at the job make sure that they kill the whole family and kill them quickly. I totally get that the advent of humans who build fences has radically interfered with elephant ecology. There used to be natural population control based on the amount of water and food available over the unbelievably huge distances that define the elephants' normal range. There was also less pressure on the vegetation when the elephants could feed over a huge area. But I don't think humans know enough about elephant society to identify and isolate a whole family, nor enough about elephant communications to say that these killings have no effect. There has been some research in elephant birth control that looks promising but so far is difficult to administer to large enough numbers to do much good. For now, the South African government has bowed to international pressure and stopped the culling. Debbie is disgusted that these foreign conservation groups have so much influence on policy but never see the results of the policy up close.

After breakfast, even though it is still chilly and damp, I head for the river path. I really enjoy being on my own for awhile and walk as far as is possible along the river. I still don't find any big animals, but I do see birds and a butterfly poses very nicely for me. It turns out later to be surprisingly hard to identify.

Above right: *African common white belenois, maybe.*
Left: *Hadedah ibis*
Right: *Jameson's firefinch*
Below right and left: *Rhinos in the late afternoon sun.*

We spend the middle of the day holed up in our tent, huddled under covers trying to stay warm.

For the evening drive, the rain finally lets up and it is possible to be almost comfortable under the poncho with the hot water bottle in my lap. Except that every time I see something exciting and start shooting pictures, it falls off. I spend an inordinate amount of time adjusting everything.

We find four rhinos close to the road, accompanied by the small bright spot of color of a Cape glossy starling. The rhinos are maybe 20 feet away and slowly make their way closer as we sit there. It is magical. We are the only truck there and we sit spellbound and quiet as the rhinos graze peacefully right next to us. They are bathed in the golden late afternoon light and the only sound is the tearing of grass.

Someone asks Debbie later why no one else was there, as most of the big animal sightings have attracted lots of attention. There was a veritable traffic jam near the leopard we saw the first day we were here. She says there is an internet bulletin board that all the guides post to so that everybody knows where the animals are. Except for the rhinos—they aren't allowed to post rhino sightings. In fact, they don't even speak about rhino sightings, hoping in some small measure to help keep the rhinos safe from poaching. We have seen the anti-poaching unit go zooming by in their truck, but never heard a scrap of information as to what they were doing. They keep their activities secret. If they encounter poachers, they shoot to kill. If they recover rhino horns, or even if a rhino dies of natural causes, they take the horns and lock them away somewhere secret.

Left: *Pygmy (also called dwarf) mongooses.*

Below: *Verreaux's (also called giant) eagle-owl*

A little way down the road, we find pygmy mongooses living in and playing on a big termite mound. They are each about 8 to 12 inches long, including their tail. We watch them basking in the last of the afternoon sun, playing and grooming, looking sleek and silky.

Then we find a Verreaux's eagle-owl, a rare and big bird. He stands about 2 feet high and looks impressive even all rumpled up from sleep. I wish we could see him fly—his wingspan is somewhere around 5 feet—but it is too early yet for him to be hunting. (I say "he" advisedly—females are even bigger.) Not much light for a picture, too much light for him to be awake yet.

Of course there is the usual assortment of animals. I am getting blasé already? Nah. The animals may be common for this area but they still are a kick to see.

Left: *Two warthogs scamper away, tails held high.*
Below left: *A female impala*
Below right: *A kudu browsing*
Bottom: *A young Cape buffalo*

Above left: *Dark-capped bulbul*

Above top: *Cape glossy starling*

Above middle: *Plumaria growing in camp.*

Above right: *Laughing dove*

Left: *Yellow-billed hornbill with a tasty morsel.*

Right: *Magpie Shrike*

Above: *An elephant amid the thorns.*

Left: *A mama warthog*

Right: *A giraffe's tongue is about 20 inches long, blue and gooey.*

ABOVE: *With the cessation of the rain there is a spectacular sunset.*

The frogs are LOUD tonight. There is a hyena somewhere near our tent. His call starts out with a low pitched "wooooo" and then a quick scoop up in pitch, ending with a short sharp "wop". There is another one who says, "gerrrrrrrrrrrrrwop." Or maybe it is the same guy saying two different things.

Chapter 5

Lisbon falls and ferns

October 1st

We travel back to Johannesburg today, to spend another night at the Outlook Lodge. While packing I discover that the insulin that I put in the refrigerator to protect it from 105° temperatures has frozen. I remember vaguely that frozen insulin is a bad thing but I have no access to any information. I stick it in my suitcase and hope that I'll be able to get online in Johannesburg and find out something.

A.D. is driving again and Andy and Gilliam are traveling with us. We stop for breakfast in a small, used to be mining town now turned tourist attraction. I order pancakes and get some chicken and spinach rolled in a thick crepe. Hmm—not quite what I had in mind, but tasty anyway. Conversation at breakfast flows as easily as usual and I enjoy the company very much.

We are taking The Panoramic Route, stopping in several places to admire the scenery. The light in the middle of the day isn't particularly interesting, but I dutifully get out at the various stops and take pictures that look just like postcards. There are lots of tourists and tour buses. Definitely not my thing. On the other hand, it gives us a chance to see a little more more of the countryside.

Beautiful Lisbon Falls!

Spectacular view from God's Window!

At the last stop there is a shopping opportunity for handcrafted things—the first I've encountered—and I happily wander down the rows of little booths looking at carvings, cloth, and bowls. Everything is brightly colored and cheerfully crowded together on the ground. It is hard to tell where one seller leaves off and another begins but they are all eager to help. One man explains that the carvings are all done locally. Another takes down and unfolds every piece of cloth I touch. I am a little embarrassed—I'm not going to buy that much—but the seller tells me not to worry, he is happy doing his job, so I stop fussing. I buy a few things and am enjoying myself until I realize that the four men are sitting in the van waiting for me and looking bored and impatient. Oops.

It is lovely to be back at Outlook Lodge where our room is clean and warm. And there is a shower—the height of luxury. But the Wi-Fi is down so there is no insulin information available.

October 2nd

We are leaving early for our flight to Durban. The Wi-Fi is back up but excruciatingly slow. I am frantically searching for information about frozen insulin while we wait for our ride to the airport. I can find little to the point. As far as I can tell, in the admittedly brief time I have to look, there has been no research and nobody really knows anything. I decide that since nothing has precipitated out of the solution, I'll go ahead and use it. The thought of trying to go to a clinic and trying to get a prescription filled is just too horrible to contemplate.

The Johannesburg airport is confusing; it takes us a while to figure out how to get our boarding passes, but people are helpful. Going through security is much easier than at a US airport—no removing shoes, segregating liquids, or taking the laptop out. A security person asks to see if there is anything under my hat, so I take it off. We smile at each other at the absurdity of it all.

The flight to Durban is short and uneventful except that I have an aisle seat and can't see when we are about to land which I find nerve-wracking. We are met at the airport by Yvette, who works for Thula Thula, and her dad who is helping her out by driving. It takes two hours to drive to Thula Thula. The first hour or so is on a well-maintained freeway. We stop several times to pay tolls. The air is clear and the countryside green. After we get off the freeway we drive through agricultural lands and then through the town of Empangeni, which looks like any small town anywhere, with car dealerships, fast food, a sign for the library off the main road. The streets are lined with trees, which have not leafed out yet. Most of the buildings are made of red brick. There is plenty of traffic and lots of people strolling on the sidewalks, or waiting at the bus stops. Once through the town the roads quickly deteriorate to poorly maintained tracks of potholes. We drive past the dusty, sleepy village of Buchanana. There are not many people about. I notice a medical clinic in a large, rundown, drab yellow building. (I so hope I do not have to go there.) There are several trucking businesses and other industrial concerns along the road. The surrounding vegetation is dry and dingy grey, coated with the ubiquitous dust. Goats and chickens scrounge for food amongst the litter lining the road.

Finally we arrive, check in at the main house and transfer to a truck to go to the tent camp. There are two places to stay at Thula Thula, the tent camp and the lodge. Accommodations at the tent camp are, um, tents, but very fancy ones. Accommodations at the lodge are free-standing chalets. Food at the tent camp is a mix of western and South African plain cooking. Food at the lodge is fancy French gourmet. We will be splitting our time between the two. It turns out Yvette is filling in as manager of the tent camp. She helps us get settled and proves to be wonderfully friendly and a treasure trove of information. We are too late to go on the evening game drive, so we settle into our beautiful fancy tent to rest before dinner. It is spacious, airy and comfortable. There is room to set up the computer. There is an en suite bathroom. I am very glad to be here.

Thula Thula means peace and tranquility in Zulu.

Chapter 6

October 3rd

We go for a bush walk this morning. I mention not being allowed to go on the Kruger walk, but the rangers assure me that all their guests who want to go can go and that they will be happy to match my pace. And they do. There are three of us and a guide, plus a second guide with a rifle. It is early and not too warm. There is beautiful, soft light and many invisible birds. It is difficult for me to keep up, especially going downhill, but one of the guides is very sweet about helping me and nobody seems to mind waiting for me. I am concentrating so hard on not falling down that I miss almost all of the stories and only retain one joke. (The younger ranger said his mother thought he was so hot that she called him son.) We get fairly close to a family of giraffes: dad, mom and baby. They really are big when you are standing on the ground.

We laze around most of the day. There are some nyala grazing in the meadow in front of the camp and baboons in the trees behind the camp. We sit in the large open-air veranda that serves as sitting room, dining room and bar. It is also where Wi-Fi is available, so Robert spends the day online. It has a tin roof which makes a startling amount of noise when a troop of vervet monkeys runs across it. We can see the branches of the big tree near the veranda bounce and bend as the monkeys use them for springboards on and off the roof.

Then some baboons join them and they all thunder across the roof. It sounds like hundreds of animals. There are probably eight total. It is hard to tell as they are moving fast in their game of chase. I also can't tell who is chasing whom—I think they trade off. Then the little dog Tonic (his brother, who lives at the main house, is named Gin, of course) starts barking at them and chaos ensues until the monkeys and baboons go their separate ways.

LEFT: *Vervet monkey*

Top: *A nyala in front of our tent.*

Above: *It is fun walking with Tonic as he alerts whenever there are animals near. I see nyala and baboons I would have missed on my own.*

Right: *I hear and then finally see a go-away bird. I've been hearing and trying to see this bird since we got to Kruger. Its official name is a lourie and its call sounds like a snooty old maid with a Greta Garbo attitude talking into a paper towel roll.*

The little swimming pool looks inviting as the weather has turned warm again. But the water is so cold, it is hard to catch my breath. I manage to get wet, walk across the shallow end and I'm done. I use the outside shower behind our tent to rinse off the chlorine. It has a beautiful and private view of the bush. The wind has come up and is cold, but the water is hot, so my shower is comfortable and refreshing. I am relaxed enough afterward to take a long and luxurious nap. After a while Robert returns with the computer and I spend the rest of the afternoon working on downloading and editing pictures.

We go for our first Thula Thula game drive this evening. The ranger/guide/driver's name is Cameron and the ranger/guide/spotter is Victor. Victor sits on a jump seat attached to the front bumper of the truck and is responsible for interpreting tracks and finding animals. I am a bit surprised at first that we have two people—after all, Debbie did just fine by herself. But after only a few minutes on the horrible roads I understand why it would be hard for one person to look for animals and at the same time drive over the ruts, rocks, potholes, washouts, twists, 45° slopes, thorny shrubs close to the road, thorny trees close overhead, downed trees left in the road by the elephants and other such impediments to safe travel.

Left: *We all have to climb out while Victor supervises and Cameron drives the truck through a thorny tree limb blocking the road and too big to move.*

Above: *White-faced whistling ducks*

Below: *A luna moth. I am impressed that Victor is able to spot it as we drive by. It is well camouflaged.*

We see signs of elephants—poop and prints—but no elephants. Victor and Cameron put a lot of effort into trying to figure out where they have gone, jumping out of the truck several times to read the elephants' tracks and driving to the most likely spots. The rangers do make a point of saying that if the elephants don't want to be found, they won't be. It is amazing how many elephant shaped trees and bushes there are that turn out to not be elephants.

ABOVE: *Looking for this...*

RIGHT: *...and finding this.*

At dusk we go to Gwala Gwala Dam where Lawrence Anthony's ashes were scattered. The water is low now so stumps are sticking out. There are big trees in the middle of the water filled with birds and many more birds on the shore. I know there are ibis because their call is distinctive and I ask. Beyond that there isn't enough light to identify or photograph any of them. I want to come back here in the daylight and spend more time.

Black-crowned tchagra

Chapter 7

October 4th

Today it is just Robert and me on our morning walk, so the rangers are able to tailor the trip more closely to my capabilities (or lack thereof). We don't go as far or for as long, but where we go is beautiful. We walk off the road and follow an elephant path into a small secluded valley, hidden away from casual visitors. (Ok, they probably take everybody here, but for today anyway it is just us.)

It is quiet, except for bits of bird song that Seeya identifies for us. He teaches us words for each song that make it easier to remember who is who. "I am a red-eyed dove" follows the cadence of the red-eyed dove's call. The African mourning dove says, early in the morning, "Work harder" and later in the afternoon

LEFT: *Seeya and Saynella (at least that's what their names sound like) are the rangers who have taken us on our bushwalks so far.*

RIGHT: *The animal path leading to the hidden valley.*

"Drink lager." There is another bird I haven't managed to see, whose name I never did get, who beeps like a demented dump truck backing up. Seeya says it is easy to hear and very hard to see—so I guess I'm right on track with this one. There is a crowned hornbill that sounds disconcertingly like a goat.

We see a wildebeest, also known as a gnu. To Robert's intense disappointment we do not see agnother gnu. We do enjoy chuckling about it though. (If you don't get this joke, go to iTunes and listen to The Gnu by Flanders and Swann.)

LEFT: *A blue gnu. (Really.) There are also black gnus which have white tails and are now found only where they have been deliberately bred in specific parks. Legend has it that the gnu was built from the leftovers after God finished with all the other animals. It has the face of a mule, the beard of a goat, the horns of a cow, and the body of a horse.*

A big group of people from Durban, Australia and Devon, England arrives this morning, so my customized morning walks may be at an end. I have enjoyed them immensely. The ranger with the rifle is a constant reminder that it is dangerous out in the bush, but I love being more connected than is possible in a truck. It surprises me to realize how happy I am here. Probably because I am being waited on hand and foot, well fed, totally entertained and periodically taken out for exercise.

A new couple arrives this afternoon, Dave and Marie from Houston. The first thing Marie wants to know is when the tusks were removed from the rhinos. It is hard to know what to say to that. Dave is sharp with her and doesn't hesitate to tell everyone how stupid she is. They have come to Thula Thula straight from their 30 hour flight and there is a rumor that he flew business class while she was stuck in economy, so he was comfortable enough to sleep on the plane and she wasn't. They disappear into their tent to sleep and we don't see them for the rest of the day.

Above: *Crowned hornbill*

On this evening's drive we see elephants! The first one we meet is a 24 to 25-year-old bull elephant named Mabula. He is usually by himself as befits a bull elephant of his age, but today he is with the herd. He comes VERY close. So close I could touch him, except that seems like a bad idea. So close I can only see one eye in the camera. He looks right at me with his big soft liquid dark eye. I put down the camera to look at him and he slowly winks at me and we smile at each other. To be acknowledged by such a creature is a moment I will tuck away in my heart forever.

Above: *Mabula is a beautiful young tusker and he knows it. His demeanor is the elephantine equivalent of a Wall Street Master of the Universe.*

Left: *So it turns out the corn is really, really high.*

Mabula looks us over leisurely, and then, having satisfied his curiosity about the humans in the truck, melts away silently into the bush. Is there such a thing as exhilarating tranquility? That would describe my first close up encounter with a wild elephant.

We hear the rest of the herd in the shrubby forest near the road, breaking off branches and crunching through the underbrush. They are noisy! In fact, they sound just like a herd of elephants. Then they all slowly amble into the open, heading for a drink at Gwala Gwala dam. Cameron says it is unusual for Nana, the matriarch, and Frankie, the second in command, to show their young babies to visitors, but they do for us. What a treat! We watch mesmerized as they move in front of us into the forest on the other side. Then we follow the road to the dam and get there in time to watch them come back out into the open.

Above: *Nana with two of her offspring.*

Right: *The herd crossing the road. Note the baby surrounded and protected by everybody.*

Below right and left: *An adolescent.*

There are bones at the dam belonging to the one elephant Lawrence had to put down. An adolescent member of the herd picks up one of the bones and holds it, then sets it on the ground and gently rolls it around. This is normal elephant behavior (though it is unusual to get to see it) and nobody really knows why they do it. Giraffes chew on bones for calcium, but I'm pretty sure they don't care whose bones they are. The elephants ignore the bones of other species and treat elephant bones with respect.

When they finish drinking, the elephants wander off and suddenly they are gone. After all the noise they made earlier it is surprising that they are so quiet and just disappear.

ABOVE AND LEFT: *Two adolescents take turns touching an elephant femur.*

Right: *This big guy, around four years old, is still suckling. It looks ridiculous—he can barely get down low enough to drink.*

Above: *Tusks become visible at two to three years of age and continue growing thoughout an elephant's life.*

ABOVE AND BELOW: *Nana's baby is named Lolo. She is two months old and weighs about 250 pounds.*

Above: *On the way back to camp we see a brown-hooded kingfisher. He is about eight inches tall.*

Below: *And a KwaZulu dwarf chameleon, about three inches long..*

We have dinner in the boma. The term boma originally referred to a livestock enclosure, but in this case it is an open air dining area with a fire pit, buffet tables and two grills. We eat Roman senator style, seated around three sides of the camp fire. There are candles on the tables and tall torches on the perimeter fence. It should be beautiful and romantic, but I can't see in the flickering sparking glare. The table is too spread out to be friendly and there is little food that I can eat. Somehow they forget to offer us anything to drink. Robert has brought a bottle of water with him, so we finish that off. He says he has overheard someone ordering lemonade, so I finally get up, gingerly walk over to a server (it would be nice not to fall flat on my face—I cannot see a thing) and ask for some. It is lemon flavored tonic water, carbonated and horribly sweet. Undrinkable. Dessert is good. I have no clue what it is—a brown sugary cakey thing with a thin sauce. That is basically all I get for dinner.

This is not as congenial a group as Kruger. The dining set up isn't as conducive to general socializing and there is no Chatty Cathy to oil the wheels of conversation and bind the group together in a commonality of annoyance.

ABOVE: *Lolo*

Chapter 8

October 5th

On today's morning walk we see wild rosemary and vibrant purple verbena (a plant I could actually identify). There is a funnel spider who comes running out of her hole whenever her web is disturbed. The spider is just a bit bigger than a quarter. Robert spots a hinged-shell tortoise making his way alongside the path. This is a rare sighting—Robert is getting good at this game. The tortoise is about a foot long.

ABOVE: *Funnel spider*
ABOVE LEFT AND LEFT: *Hinge-shelled tortoise.*

We pass the water pump and pipe which is the main source of water for the camp and lodge. There is a big concrete lid sitting on top of the round concrete barrier that protects the pump and pipe, a lid that takes 12 men to shift into place and one elephant to remove completely. The elephants like to take the lid off, break the pipe and play in the resulting fountain and mud hole. The camp goes without water when they do. The rangers came up with the solution of surrounding the well with sharp pointy fist-sized rocks, which keep the elephants away because they do not like to walk on sharp things. I look at it and wonder why they don't just move the rocks with their trunks. The rangers shrug and say so far it is working.

The tree outside our tent has many dark red flowers. It is called a weeping boa bean tree. It leaks sap—which I have not seen—and its seed pods can be ground up for ersatz coffee. Victor says the "coffee" is really bad.

We see Dave briefly at breakfast rounding up some food for Marie. He is back and forth several times, making sure she gets what she needs, worried that she might be getting sick.

During today's evening drive, we are chased by Mabula. He is just coming into musth, a potentially dangerous situation, though he is still being relatively sane.

ABOVE: *Weeping boa bean tree*
OPPOSITE: *Mabula stopping for a nibble.*

MUSTH

Musth is a periodic condition of bull elephants marked by increased secretions from the temporal glands and very high testosterone levels. An elephant in musth is unpredictably aggressive and dangerously violent. Understandably, musth is difficult to study and not much scientific information is available. It is not well understood what causes musth nor how or if it relates to reproduction. It is known that in African elephants it starts when an elephant is around 25 years old and can last one to two months at a time. How often it occurs is not clear. The presence of an older male can inhibit the younger males from going into musth. It is speculated that the swelling of the temporal glands causes severe discomfort and contributes to the animal's meanness and hair-trigger temper. It is amazing how little is really known about elephant physiology, psychology, and family life.

Mabula has become protective of the herd and is obviously trying to keep us away. We are in an open vehicle and Cameron drives as well (and as fast) backward as he does forward. So we are speeding backward over a very rough track and the elephant just keeps coming and keeps coming. Just when it seems that disaster is inevitable, Mabula stops and grabs a nibble off a nearby tree, showing an insouciance for which I am very grateful.

The rangers say that if he were really angry he could easily overtake and overturn the truck. Even at his most friendly, he gets my adrenaline going. I'm not exactly afraid…

I looked up some elephant statistics yesterday. An average African adult male elephant stands 10 to 13 feet at the shoulder and weighs somewhere around 15,000 pounds. In other words, HUGE. African elephants are the largest land animal, which didn't mean much to me until I got close to one. Adrenalin mixed with a little fear seems like a reasonable response.

But, oh, what a gorgeous creature he is!

Dinner is set up so that the big group is eating at their own table and we are at a separate table with Dave and Marie. Dave works for Chevron and travels all over the world. He is here for a conference in Cape Town and Marie has come along for the ride. She is a chemistry teacher at a community college and does fundraising for an animal shelter in their small town just outside of Houston. She and I have a good time swapping animal rescue stories. She is reading Mitchener's *Centennial*, which I have read, and given the setting, it makes for an interesting discussion. Dave keeps trying to shut her up saying she talks too much. At the same time, he is gracious about interpreting for her as she is quite hard of hearing. Fortunately, he finally relaxes and the conversation becomes general. Everybody has such interesting stories to tell, we sit talking for a long time. Marie's inane remarks from yesterday were apparently the result of jet lag. Tonight she is perfectly together and a delight to talk to. I am glad once more that we got jet lag out of the way at the Outlook Lodge, where zero social interaction was required of us. I enjoy the dinner immensely.

ABOVE: *Mabula*

Mabula comes to visit

Chapter 9

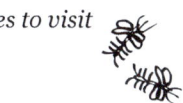

October 6th

I don't sleep well and have bad dreams—something about very sharp points on tightly wrapped white boxes (relating to the water pipe and pump?)—the little I do sleep. I watch the sunrise and hear the world wake up. A baboon barks and the birds start calling. A vervet monkey plays in the tree outside our front door and nyala graze beside the tent.

The monkeys are out on the lawn this morning while we have our hot chocolate before going on our walk. It is fun to watch Robert watching them watching him.

Above: *Early morning vervet monkey.*
Left: *Early morning Robert.*

This morning's bush walk, led again by Seeya and Saynella, is with the big group of people (though Dave and Marie don't show up) and it is too long for me. We are out for over two hours and my legs are wobbly by the end. But I only fall once and that is just a sudden sit down while trying to negotiate a narrow dry stream, no harm done. So I survive.

We walk up a dry river bed which has footprints from giraffes, zebras, nyalas and elephants in the sand. I see clearly a yellow fronted bee-eater (called a small bee-eater in my bird book). The joke being, of course, that it only eats yellow-fronted bees. (Or small bees if you go by my book.)

I also take a picture of a bird not identified by the rangers. According to my book, it is a chinspot battis. Such a lovely outlandish name.

There are lots of birds evident by their calls, but as always, difficult to see. Plus it is a large group of people today and noisy—not conducive to birding.

Above: *Small bee-eater*
Right: *Chinspot battis*

We come across the skull of a zebra. Seeya says he can tell it was a male zebra because there are two extra front tooth sockets separated a little from the rest of the front teeth. These are for canine teeth and male zebras can evidently get quite aggressive with them. I remember reading in *Guns, Germs and Steel*, by Jared Diamond, that zebras were not domesticated because they bite and they don't let go. I don't think he mentioned the canine teeth, but it all fits.

ABOVE: *Zebra skull showing the tooth sockets*

ALL YOU EVER WANTED TO KNOW ABOUT POOP

Possibly More

(Mercifully, no pictures)

Here is the scoop on poop. Elephants walk as they poop and their poop is tinged orange from the tannin in the bark they eat. Rhino poop is black and they stand still, so it tends to pile high. It has a strong, distinctive, albeit indescribable, odor. Buffalo make cow patties (duh) and hippo poop smells fishy, though they are strict vegetarians. Hippos use their tails like windshield wipers to splatter poop around to mark their territory. (I saw this once at the San Francisco zoo when I was young. The hippo's name was Puddles, the mess was considerable and I remember it vividly.) Hippos also make piles to serve as navigational aids when they are out of the river at night. Like Hansel and Gretel's breadcrumbs. Sort of.

Hyenas have white poop from the calcium in the bones they eat. Their poop works well as a chalk substitute, should you be out in the bush and need one.

Giraffes' poop is small for the size of the animal and flattened from falling from such a big height.

There is a spitting game played with the small hard pellets of kudu and impala poop. It requires a certain skill (?) to hold the poop pellet in your mouth long enough to maximize the distance you can spit it but minimize the risk that it will disintegrate. At Thula Thula, we watched the ranger Seeya spit a pellet a truly amazing distance. He tried to talk Robert and me into trying it. He did not succeed. Yuck is all I have to say about it.

The rangers talk about how the Zulus use various shrubs but I can't keep track of which is what. One is for cleaning your teeth, one is for keeping mosquitoes away, one makes a good camp pillow. The thorns on the various plants are astonishing—short and barbed, long and lethal, and everything in between. More verbena is blooming, making a striking carpet of bright purple.

While we are walking, the wind comes up and we get a few spits of rain. Now, just before lunch, the wind is coming in big gusts that I can hear starting at the far end of the valley, coming on like a locomotive. It makes the tent flap, shudder and thunder. The clouds have gotten thicker and darker, but no significant rain yet. Our picnic lunch in the bush has been canceled.

This afternoon, Mabula comes by the camp to check things out. Dave, Marie, Robert and I go down into the meadow to see him. I take lots of pictures but am concerned when I can't tell which side of the elephant wire he is on. This wire encircles the whole camp and has enough electricity running through it to kill a man and to mildly inconvenience an elephant, so it is conceivable that Mabula has decided to ignore it. I back up in a hurry (which admittedly would not have done me much good anyway) but in fact Mabula has chosen to stay on his side of the wire. He looks us over, nibbles on some bushes, and wanders off.

Above: *The elephant wire comes off the top of the pole to go across the road and is high enough for the trucks to go under, while still being effective in discouraging the elephants from joining us for dinner.*

Left: *Mabula checks us out and enjoys a snack. The wire is visible just in front of the bottom of his ear.*

This evening we see a giraffe family. In fact, we see lots of giraffes. They are so laid back and goofy looking, it is hard to remember that they are actually dangerous, that one kick from a hind leg is powerful enough to kill a lion.

From the top: *Dad, mom, and a youngster who is standing conveniently close to his mom for size comparison.*

We also see a large herd of zebras, with two young colts. The babies are born with legs as long as the adults, making them hard to see when in the herd and protecting them from predation. And then there are all the zebra jokes, although I can only remember one: which side of a zebra has the most stripes? The outside, of course.

Above: *A young zebra.*

Middle: *The largest herd we've seen so far.*

Right: *The light brown on top of the white stripes is characteristic of Burcell's zebras, the most common species of zebra and the only kind we see.*

We catch sight of the old bull, Gobisa. Not a member of the original herd, he was brought in as a mentor and role model for the younger bulls. Young bulls are kicked out of the matriarchal herd when they are teenagers. They form loose associations with other bulls and learn how to behave from the older ones. Mabula did not have anyone to show him the ropes or even just to hang out with when he was forced out of the herd and he had a rough and lonely time. It is thought that Gobisa came too late to help him much and they don't get along very well. At least now there are other younger bull elephants he can be with. Gobisa isn't around the others much and is rarely seen.

Above: *Gobisa, the elder statesman of the herd.*

Right: *The herd crossing the road with the littlest in the middle as usual.*

Next Page: *Mabula*

Mabula does not like us getting close and gives chase again. This time when he stops he curls up his trunk and rests his forehead against a big tree and tries to push it over. The tree sways but does not break and Mabula gives up. Cameron is wary of this behavior, saying that it is possible that he could get dangerously angry at not being able to break the tree and we are lucky that he doesn't seem to care.

potato vine plant

Chapter 10

October 7th

On today's morning walk, it is just the two of us and Victor. We follow an elephant path replete with new footprints and fresh poop. We are outside the wire and it makes me nervous, but Victor undoubtedly knows what he is doing. It is a part of the bush we haven't seen before. The path goes along the edge of a small ravine. The grass along the path is tall and green, the ravine is a lush palette of green leaves and grasses, mixed with the red, orange and gray barks of the trees.

Right: *There are approximately 1700 different species of native trees in South Africa. That's as far as I can get identifying this one.*

We find a bees' nest, a potato vine plant, a dung beetle that scurries away before I can get a picture, and wood borer nymphs as thick as my thumb feasting on an elephant-damaged tree stump (eww). We also, evidently, see a toothbrush tree, as I have a picture of Victor demonstrating its use. There is no way I could identify this tree on my own, though this is the second or third time it has been pointed out. To my relief, we don't see any elephants.

Above: *A freshly splintered tree trunk, evidence of recent elephant activity.*

Above right: *Victor brushes his teeth, Zulu bush style.*

Right: *Wood borer nymphs enjoy the fruits of the elephants' labor. Eww, again.*

Opposite page: *One view of the village of Buchanana with new construction going on in the foreground.*

Today we visit a Zulu Sangoma, a village wise woman, in the nearby village of Buchanana. There are six of us going: Robert and me, Dave and Marie, and two young female journalists from France. Victor is our driver for today. We drive through the village on dirt roads lined with a startling and distressing amount of trash. Each compound is about the size of a big suburban lot fenced off with a hodgepodge of fencing materials. A brief inspection shows chicken wire, cast iron railings, corrugated tin, tree trunks, clothes lines and thin sticks woven together. The dirt inside each compound is mostly swept clean, but no one seems to care about the plastic bags and bottles and other litter lining the roads and blown onto the outside of the fences.

Each lot has several small structures, mostly the iconic round thatched huts called rondavels, though there are some shanty shacks and some modern, albeit small, stucco houses as well. Various levels of prosperity and poverty are represented. From Thula Thula it is possible to see the lights of the village at night. Robert asks how the electricity is paid for as there are no meters in evidence. It turns out that there are coin-fed meters inside each home, so electricity is dispensed on a pay-as-you-go basis.

Top: *A more prosperous part of the village.*

Middle: *The village store.*

Left: *The post office is a major feature on the main road.*

On the main road are several construction businesses and a medical clinic. There is also a primary school in the village, though the older children are bussed to school in Empangeni, about 20 miles away. I love watching the people. Most of the women, mostly of "traditional" build, wear wonderfully bright, complex clothes, mixing hot pinks with purples, yellows and greens with orange, just about every color you can imagine with every other color, mixing plaids, stripes, prints and solids, and including pleats, ruffles, gathers and layers wherever and however possible. I wish I could get a closer look because the layers and construction are not immediately obvious. I don't want to offend anyone, so I don't ask, and don't take pictures, either. Of course, there are the people who opt for sweatpants and hoodies, comfortable but not nearly as interesting. Most of the men wear plaid or striped oxford shirts tucked into neatly pressed chinos. The children wear either school uniforms or brightly colored polo shirts and jeans. All the people we saw were well groomed and all of the clothes were spotlessly clean and ironed. Even on the kids. Even the sweatpants and hoodies. Given the dusty dirt roads and the small primitive houses, this seems to be quite a feat.

ABOVE: *Two little kids play in their yard. There is no visible supervision other than the dogs, but the compound is completely enclosed and gated. The woven structure on the left is a chicken coop.*

Above: *The Sangoma's grandson. He is shy, but willing to have his picture taken.*

Right: *The Sangoma's daughter. She helps organize the things her mother needs for our session.*

Below: *A milk cow grazing by the side of the road.*

Opposite page: *In the rondavel of the Sangoma.*

There are cows, chickens and goats running free everywhere. They graze where they can, sleep in the middle of the road if it suits them, have the right of way and know it and, in general, are small but look healthy enough.

There are also dogs in most of the compounds. Victor tells us that they are kept for security and not as pets. They don't look friendly. Marie has to be bodily restrained from petting them.

The Sangoma, a middle-aged plump woman, is sitting in the middle of her stone rondavel when we arrive. After we remove our shoes, we are ushered by Victor through a low wooden door (even I had to duck) and sit on reed mats around the perimeter of the concrete floor. The rondavel is about fifteen feet in diameter with one small window covered by a wooden shutter. The one door is left open to provide a little bit of light. The walls are painted robin egg blue, though not recently, and the floor is a dark red. There are bags of unidentifiable stuff by the door to our right and canisters of powders and herbs to our left. I also notice various odd things stored in the roof amongst the thatch—an umbrella, a sieve, ropes, a small mattock.

The Sangoma is dressed in a vivid red dress with a leopard skin print top, covered by a bright white open coat. She kneels on a reed mat in the center facing away from the light coming through the door. She lights a candle and incense and then starts deep belly yells which reverberate off the walls. Some are short barks, others are long howls. They are all so loud that they hurt my ears. After a while—it seems like a long while—she starts breaking up the yells with rhythmic chanting. It sounds like lists of names, though I don't ask and don't actually know that. (We were told ahead of time that her job is to communicate with ancestors.) I start recognizing repetitions. While she is yelling and chanting, she swishes around a scepter made from the end hairs of a black wildebeest's tail, sometimes flicking it over her shoulder, sometimes tapping the butt end on the floor while she leans down and mutters. I take pictures, having received permission in advance, but afterward find that most of them are disturbing to look at. Her eyes show her to be in a trance, totally absorbed in her ritual.

After another eternity, she begins talking to each of us in turn. Victor translates from the Zulu. As Robert points out afterward, she offers mostly platitudes but that is fine with me. I'm sure she could tell me things I don't want to hear. She tells everyone but me that they are being watched over by the angels of specific ancestors, like a grandmother for one of the French girls. She also tells one of the French girls that

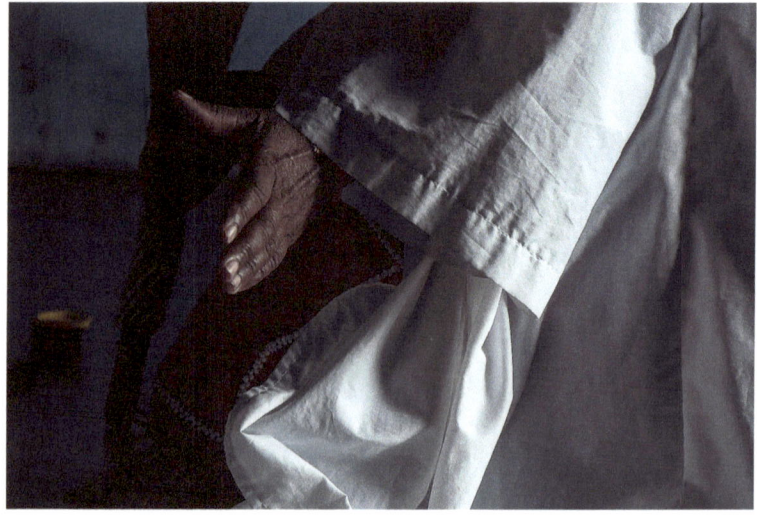

she should go home and get married. That provokes a lot of embarrassed laughter, as the girl has a live-in boyfriend and hopes he is the one she is supposed to marry. The Sangoma asks Robert if he has back problems (he doesn't) and tells him that when he met me his life changed significantly and for the better (well, I should hope so). She tells Dave that his joints are bothering him and that Marie is good for him. Easy guesses for older men, both obviously on marriage #2. To me she says nothing about ancestors, or health, or anything else except that my family will watch out for me and take care of me and (as she says to everyone) everything will be fine. It would be interesting to hear what she would say in a more private communion with the ancestors.

Once she finishes with her predictions and comes out of her trance, she takes off her white coat and gets her own eyes back. She poses for pictures with a mischievous smile and bright eyes. I like this woman. She works hard at her job and I feel from her a great deal of compassion, even for us ignorant tourists.

Top: *The Sangoma's hands were eloquent during the ritual.*
Above: *The Sangoma, relaxing after her hard work.*
Left: *She holds my hand as we pose for pictures.*

The elephants are waiting to welcome us when we return. We see Frankie with one of her older calves and Nana with her baby. Mabula is hanging out with some of the younger bulls and doesn't hassle us for once. Victor says it is unusual for the elephants to be near the entrance. I am thrilled that they have come to meet us.

ABOVE AND RIGHT:
Nana and baby Lolo.

While we were visiting the village, our luggage was moved from the tent camp over to a chalet at the lodge. Though I think I will miss the outdoorsy experience of the tent, the lodge is certainly as beautiful. It is in a park-like setting with big trees and a green lawn, fertilized and mowed compliments of the two hand-reared orphaned rhinos who call this home. The rhinos are named Thabo, the male, and Ntombi, the female. They are very difficult to tell apart without getting a little more up close and personal than I really want to. Our room is spacious and airy, complete with the two rhinos sleeping in the dusty hollow that they have made right outside our door.

ABOVE AND RIGHT: *Rhinos taking a late morning nap.*

There are posted rules all over the place about how to behave around the rhinos, including not going close, not making noise, and not doing anything to draw their attention. Because the first two rhinos brought to Thula Thula were killed by poachers, these rhinos are accompanied by an armed guard 24/7. Their handler, Alyson, who bottle fed them when they were babies, is also in attendance when the rhinos are in or near the camps. Both humans are vigilant about keeping everybody away. When the rhinos were babies it wasn't quite such an issue, but they are almost full grown now and it is imperative for there to be no human/rhino incidents. If a human were hurt, the rhino would have to be put down. That seems unfair and Marie and I agree that it would be better to shoot the human instead—they aren't endangered. Unfortunately, that draconian approach is not what would happen. So we all follow the rules and the guard and handler stand watch. All of which means we are stuck in our cabin until the rhinos wake up and wander elsewhere. Good time for our own naps.

The rhinos decide it is time for lunch and move away from our door. We go over to the common room and meet the lodge manager Mabona, who has taken over Yvette's job of watching out for us. The food here is fancier than at the tent camp with a menu for each meal that has at least two choices each for salad, soup, entrée and dessert. Mabona goes over the menu with me to determine what I will be able to eat. For the rest of our stay either she or someone from the kitchen reviews the offerings with me and I am (finally and with a huge sigh of relief) able to find enough to eat. And the food is absolutely delicious. Well cooked, well presented. Lovely.

The sun has come out, so we sit on the veranda for our lunch. Robert tries to raise the umbrella by our table. It doesn't work. Robert, being Robert, analyses the problem, figures out what to do, and fixes it. The kitchen staff are slightly embarrassed but impressed. They say it would have been hours if not days before the maintenance people would have gotten around to it.

Top: *The view from our room.*

Right: *As we are starting out on this evening's drive we enjoy watching a male nyala visiting the tent camp.*

Feet

Giraffes have an odd gait. Rather than alternating left front, right back, right front, left back, like most ungulates, they move right front and back and then left front and back, as this picture shows. This gives them their characteristic rolling walk. Their hooves are the size of dinner plates and pack a mean punch.

Elephants walk on tip-toe and listen with their feet. They have six digits in each foot, solidly encased in fibrous, fatty tissue designed to support their tremendous weight. The five normal toes point forward and down while the extra digit points backward into the heel pad, forming an arch more closely related in structure to a human foot than to other quadrupeds. Not all the toes have nails and none of them touch the ground. Their front feet, which support 60% of their weight, are bigger and round, the back feet are smaller and oval. The soles of their feet are thick, spongy, elastic pads densely packed with cells that can detect the deep rumbling vibrations they use to communicate. (Elephants have a vocal range of 10 octaves!) Young elephants (like Mabula here) show a marked ridge pattern on their foot pads. As an elephant ages, the ridges are worn down. The highly elastic pad is what allows elephants to walk without making any noise as it smothers objects beneath it, muffling the sound.

We find giraffes drinking at one of the watering holes. Cameron spends some time looking at elephant tracks, trying to figure out where they are. It looks like they milled around in one place for awhile and it is hard to tell where they went after that.

Mabula surprises us, emerging out of the bush right in front of the truck. The rest of the herd is presumably nearby but we don't see any of them. Mabula gets very close and we go backward very fast. He is persistent and disconcertingly fast. The pads of his feet make a rhythmic shush-shush-shush-shush which speeds up as he runs faster. His trunk swings, his tail swings and his ears flap and frame his huge head. Fortunately he is still doing his chase, stop and nibble routine, so we are able to get away.

Above: *Mabula moving fast.*

We travel awhile on the perimeter road, which we haven't seen before. Compared to the rest of the roads, it is very well maintained to help the anti-poaching rangers, I presume. Evidently Nana and Frankie have split the herd today as we find Frankie and her offspring miles away from where we saw Mabula. As we watch Frankie amble down the road, the rangers speculate on her probable pregnancy.

When we get back to the lodge, I compliment Cameron on the great game drive, even if most of it was backwards. He laughs.

ABOVE: *Frankie*

At the dam

Chapter 11

October 8th

We go on an early morning drive today instead of a walk. Because it is just the two of us with Cameron, I am able to talk him into going to Gwala Gwala dam and spending all our time there instead of driving around. I would like to just sit and see what wildlife will show up. The dam is as good as I think it will be with many birds active in the early morning. Best of all, we see a crocodile glide through the water and pull himself up on shore. Robert and Cameron discuss Kipling's *Just So Stories* and Robert regales us with *How the Elephant Got His Trunk*.

ABOVE AND LEFT:
Weaver birds

ABOVE AND OPPOSITE PAGE:
Yellow-billed kite

Left: *African darter*

Below: *Spur-winged goose*

Bottom: *One of the three crocodiles that live at the dam.*

Above: *White-backed vulture*
Above right: *Yellow-throated longspur*
Right: *Egyptian geese*

Above and right: *Views on the way back to the lodge for breakfast.*

We spend a lazy day napping, writing, playing on the computer, and lamenting the fact that our field trips have been moved to the last few days of our visit.

The evening drive is with Dave and Marie and an older couple from Durban. His name is Dexter, I never hear hers. We see no animals, perhaps because Dexter talks on and on and on about South African politics in the 80s and 90s. (Bless Marie and her hearing difficulties—she thinks he means the 1880s and 1890s.) His voice is loud, stridently nasal and irritating. When he starts cataloging the various atrocities committed during the fight to end apartheid, I lean over and, after having to shout "Excuse me" at him several times before I can be heard, ask if we could please not discuss this right now. He finally shuts up and we continue the drive in silence. It takes a long time for my stomach to unknot and my shoulders to relax. After the drive, he apologizes to me. We sit next to them at dinner and have a pleasant meal, with no politics discussed.

ABOVE: *At least the sunset was beautiful.*

Robert notices after dinner that one of the lights is out in the common room entryway. He inveigles a spare bulb from the kitchen staff and replaces the burnt out one. Once again, the staff is slightly embarrassed but appreciative.

When we get back to our chalet, we discover that we have no water. We ask around and further discover that the entire camp has no water. The elephants have figured out how to get at and play with (i.e. break) the main water pipe. They have completely drained the storage tank. The maintenance guys are fixing it tonight and the water truck is expected tomorrow morning. Did the elephants hear my idea of how to get past the pointy rocks? Is this evidence of elephant telepathy? Coincidence? Who knows? I'm convinced I should have kept my mouth shut and my thoughts to myself.

I have noticed over the last few days that my previously frozen insulin isn't working very well. I've almost doubled my usual dose. Odd that I couldn't find that information online, but now I know. I have enough to get by until I get home.

Above: *Yellow-billed kite*

Chapter 12

October 9th

We wake up at 3:30 a.m. More accurately, we get up at 3:30 a.m. I plan to wake up later. We are leaving Thula Thula at 4 a.m. so that we can get to the gates of the HluHluwe-Imfolozi National Park when they open at 6 a.m. We are going with Dave and Marie and the two French girls again. Our guide for the day is David, the husband of Yvette. They are the owners of Flip-Flop Tours and contract with Thula Thula to take guests to the national parks in the area.

The first part of the park's name is always spelled the same and is pronounced Shoe-Shoe-way. Yvette tells me how it is pronounced, because I ask, and then it takes me awhile to remember how to say it. I have seen the second part of the name spelled at least three different ways, but regardless of the spelling, it is pronounced the way it looks. I've decided to standardize on the spelling actually used in the park.

We are first in line at the gate and proceed to the main visitors' center where we meet Aman, the park ranger who will be our guide. (Once again, I have no idea if I got his name right.) He has a long list of rules for us before we start, but I am watching weaver birds building their nests instead of listening. I have been told that the male does the nest building and if his potential mate doesn't like it, she tears it apart. All I can see are the males working very hard on the large and intricate nests.. I don't think mating season has quite started. I wish them luck.

ABOVE: *Our SANParks guide for the day.*

Left: *Weaver birds at work.*

Below: *Evidence of elephants digging for water. Other creatures benefit from their success.*

We drive across a dry sandy river bed that has been disturbed by elephants. Aman says they are able to dig through the sand to find water. As we continue further into the park, I am struck by how open and vast the countryside is. There are many wide territorial views and I am wishing that I had brought my wide angle lens. The park is a rhino sanctuary and already we have seen several rhinos. We have also seen a herd of zebras, impala, vervet monkeys, and elephants at a distance. All of this is before breakfast, and I think I might finally be awake.

Above: *There are expansive views along the ridge...*

Right: *...some include elephants.*

Left: *David lays the table for our picnic breakfast.*

Aman takes us to a playground picnic area and he and David set out a bountiful breakfast.

I offer to help, but Aman says I should just sit down and enjoy. I am there as his guest and it is his duty and pleasure as my host to serve me. I feel I have committed a Zulu faux pas, so I do just sit and enjoy and make a point of expressing my gratitude afterward.

We wander somewhat aimlessly after breakfast, until Aman gets word, via his cell phone, that there has been a cheetah sighting. Then we do what is affectionately known as a Ferrari safari, and zoom over to where the cheetah is reported to be. There is also mention of getting a bush massage driving fast over the bumpy roads. We have heard both these terms before. They seem to be safari guide stock-in-trade.

The cheetah is still there. As we watch, a whole story unfolds:

The cheetah rests at his ease in the shade of a tree.

Then he spots and starts stalking an impala grazing in a nearby glade.

The cheetah hides behind a big bush, where the impala can't see him, and neither can we. A warthog comes trotting down the hill, bumbling along with not a care in the world, until he sees the cheetah. Oh, no! He turns right around and runs back the way he came as fast as he can.

The impala (there on the right side of the picture, mid-way up, you can see him, right?) is alerted to something being wrong. He has stopped grazing and is nervously looking around but still hasn't seen or smelled the cheetah. I'm surprised he doesn't just run anyway.

We wait and wait for the cheetah to do something. I hold my camera focused and ready at the spot I think he will run to. And then he goes! Fast! By the time my brain has told my finger to push the shutter, the cheetah is seemingly gone. I think I have not gotten a picture of him, but later when I analyze the sequence carefully, I find him well hidden by the grass, (see the spots?) turning to follow the impala. My camera shoots 4 frames per second and neither the frame before this one nor the frame after this one has a cheetah in it. But even if my camera couldn't really record it, I did see the cheetah run. Wow.

We find out later that he never did catch the impala.

Everybody is so excited by this drama that it takes a little while for us all to calm down, catch our collective breaths and move on. We go to a spot overlooking the Black Imfolozi River. It is one of the few places where is is okay to get out of the truck and it is uncomfortably crowded, but the view of the river is worth it.

Someone in the crowd thinks he has spotted a black rhino. It is feasible as this park is one of the few remaining places where they are found, but it turns out that the young man is mistaken. Too bad, but not surprising—there aren't many left.

Left: *A white rhino on the beach of the Black Imfalosi River.*

Below: *Cape buffalo, cattle egrets and a giraffe enjoy the river.*

Next we go to a hide which has been built overlooking a watering hole. There is a well beaten path to it, but very few people are there today. The hide is a simple hut thatched with reeds all over the side facing the water hole. It has a narrow horizontal slit to look through and benches to sit on. It was, however, designed by a tall person. If I sit on the benches I can't see out the narrow slit, so I have to stand up and hunch over. Not very comfortable, but the view is well worth it. We watch a grey heron and a monitor lizard hunt for fish and frogs. A hyena comes to drink and to cool off. After he leaves, a family of wary and skittish nyala come down to drink. One of them is always standing guard and there is always an adult between the little ones and the hillside. When they leave, a flock of pied crows comes boldly and noisily to splash around in the water. During all of this the heron has ignored all comers and continued his vigilant hunting.

Top: *The path to the hide.*

Above: *A monitor lizard hunting.*

Above left: *A gray heron preening.*

Left: *A hyena cools off.*

Left: *The same gray heron being vigilant.*

Below left and right: *A family of nyala.*

Bottom: *Pied crows*

I could stay here all day, but people are getting hungry so we go to another picnic area for lunch. Aman and David have outdone themselves with barbecued hot dogs and sausages. It smells delicious even if I can't eat any of it. For me there is a zucchini frittata, olives that I pick out of Robert's salad, and cheesecake for dessert, which makes a very tasty meal. A baboon comes to watch us eat. His behavior isn't entirely appropriate, and the men joke that he must be lusting after the French girls. Eventually he leaves when no one gives him either food or love.

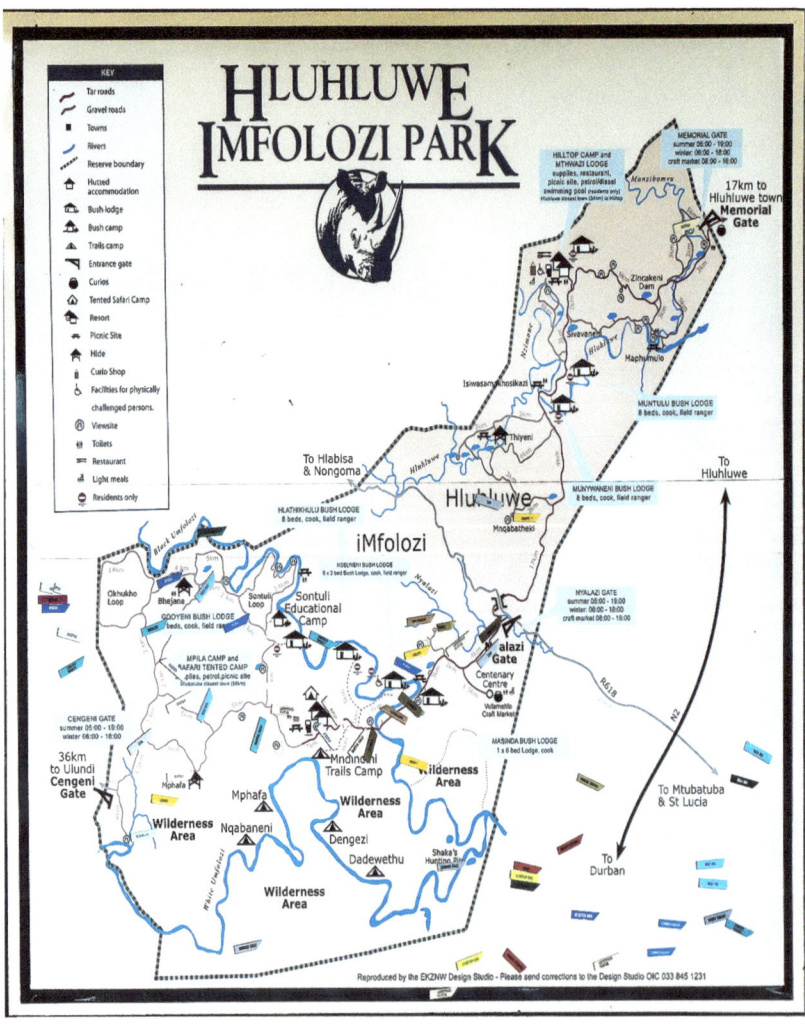

Above: *A baboon waiting to be invited to lunch.*

Left: *A large sign showing the layout of the park. The little magnetic colored tags show animal sightings people have marked for that day.*

After lunch, we continue our wanderings. We see a baby zebra, a cape buffalo who reminds me of Ferdinand, the bull in the children's book, and a nest of white-backed vultures.

ABOVE LEFT: *A young zebra being awkwardly feisty.*

ABOVE: *Just smelling the flowers.*

LEFT: *A nest of white-backed vultures. The nest was at the top of a tall tree, but the road along the ridge was at the same height as the tree.*

Then Aman gets another call on his cell. A leopard has been sighted. We can't believe our luck. We do another Ferrari safari and find the leopard resting in a sandy creek bed. I can't see him and there is a bit of frustration for both me and the guides until I figure out that there is a tree blocking my view in the back of the truck which does not affect their view in the front. Aman repositions the truck and now I can see the leopard. He is a big boy. The size of his paws is amazing. He would, in fact, be rather threatening if he weren't so sleepy. As it is, he barely moves the whole time we watch him, and we are the ones who finally must leave. I cannot move my camera angle in the truck so there is no way to take a picture of his face without the leaves in front of him.

Right and below: *Leopards are mostly nocturnal. I'm sure the gawking tourists disturbed his nap.*

We get back to Thula Thula just in time for dinner. When Cameron hears about the cheetah and leopard he declares he is green with envy. He has been a guide for a long time and has never seen either animal. I promise to show him pictures when they are processed. I don't think that makes him feel a whole lot better, but he is nice about it.

Chapter 13

October 10th

We have another field trip today. We are going to iSimangaliso Wetland Park, in Saint Lucia, a national preserve on the Indian Ocean. Again David is our driver and guide. The French girls (everybody calls them that, I don't think any disrespect is meant) have some other filming to do elsewhere so it is just Dave, Marie, Robert and me. We leave after an early breakfast, which means we get to sleep a little longer. That is much appreciated after yesterday.

On the way through Empangeni I notice the jacaranda trees in bloom. When I confirm the identity with David, he is surprised I know the name. I am pleased that I can actually recognize and name an African tree. We see more of them growing wild in Saint Lucia. At home I have only seen them growing as isolated specimens. Here they are spectacular en masse lining the streets and bursting with bright color on the hills of the wetland park.

Left: *A jacaranda tree in Saint Lucia.*

The first thing we do is go on a boat ride on what used to be an estuary and is now being called a lake because it has become completely isolated from the ocean. We see lots and lots of hippos plus the occasional crocodile (or two). The lake is shallow and muddy.

Top: *Lake Saint Lucia*

Above and Left: *These five big guys were all lurking underneath the dense overhanging branches right next to the dock.*

RIGHT: *The guide on the boat passes around a hippo tooth. Robert, of course, carries a six-inch ruler at all times.*

A few hippo facts

Hippos are vegetarians and they feed on land at night. One hippo can eat up to 150 pounds of grass per night. They weigh on average 4,000 pounds but males, who do not stop growing as they get older, can weigh up to 9,000 pounds. They are territorial in the water, each bull with his own harem in his own section of water, but they are not territorial on land. During the day they sleep in the shallows of freshwater lakes and rivers, with most of their body under water because they sunburn badly. They sweat a natural sunblock that is oily and red and keeps their skin from cracking. They cannot swim or float, so they stay in shallow water, folding their legs so that they are as completely submerged as possible. If they have to cross a deep stretch of water they walk along the bottom. They can hold their breath for about 5 minutes. They are the most dangerous animal in Africa. They can run faster than humans, are mean tempered and have a ferocious bite. In Saint Lucia, the tourists are locked in their rooms at night to keep them safe from the marauding hippos.

LEFT AND BELOW: *A giant kingfisher poses for us three feet away from the boat's bow. At about 16 inches long, he lives up to his name.*

Top: *We drift past mangrove forests.*

Above: *A crocodile nestles asleep under the mangrove trees.*

Left: *A fish eagle looking regal in a tree near the water's edge.*

Above: *Cattle egrets perch on a bush.*

Left: *A kudu outstanding in his field.*

Below: *A flock of pied avocets fly overhead.*

Above: *Yellow-billed storks*

Right: *A harem of hippos sleeps in the shallow water.*

Below left: *The smile of a crocodile.*

Below right: *Shopping in Saint Lucia.*

After our boat ride is over, David takes us to downtown Saint Lucia. There is a small open air market with booths similar to those I saw on the way from Kruger to Johannesburg. I now know that this will be my last shopping opportunity. Fortunately this time I know exactly what I want and manage to find all of it in record time. I run out of South African rands, but the sellers are happy to take US dollars. I am worried that I have mixed up the exchange rate and overpaid for my purchases, but then I decide I don't have any way to know so I don't care.

David takes us to another part of the preserve for a picnic lunch. Not as fancy as yesterday, but there is more food I can eat and I enjoy it very much. We sit under trees and I watch birds while I eat. My offer to help clean up is accepted and so I feel better as I have made some contribution to today's efforts.

Above: *My picnic bird, a yellow-bellied greenbul.*

Next we go to Estuary Beach. It is a very wide beach, a long hike to the water. The wind is blowing hard, but I am determined to put my toes in the Indian Ocean and so we make the trek. Robert cannot forbear to comment that it looks exactly like the ocean 20 minutes away from home, but really it doesn't and he goes wading anyway.

Above: *Estuary Beach looking north.*

Left: *Estuary Beach looking east. The water is cold! There is 5,000 miles (more or less) of unobstructed ocean between Saint Lucia and Perth, Australia.*

Again we arrive back at Thula Thula too late for a game drive and a little early for dinner. We wander over to the bar and are immediately offered champagne to celebrate a guest's birthday. We've never met these people before, but it feels good to be included. Victor welcomes us back and says we have been missed. The multi-talented Cameron is behind the bar pouring drinks, proving to be a congenial host and competent bartender. He modestly admits to playing rugby and discusses the game in detail and at some length with some of the guests. He knows us by now and gives Robert a cola and me a glass of water. We join in the toast to the birthday boy.

Dinner tonight is in the boma again. Victor and Cameron both sit down to eat with us and the conversation is more general than it has been at other dinners. The new guests are from Australia and Belgium. Victor demonstrates how to pick up hot coals from the fire with bare hands. Something to do with creating and maintaining a layer of ash between your hands and the hot ember. I don't think I'll be trying this at home. The kitchen staff brings in a birthday cake and sings Happy Birthday in Zulu. The cake is delicious.

Chapter 14

October 11th

It is hot today, even in the early morning. We watch vervet monkeys while we drink our pre-game drive cocoa.

We go on this morning's drive with Rudi, the birthday boy from yesterday, and his wife whose name I've never heard—what's with these wives with no names? Anyway, they are an amiable couple from Belgium.

ABOVE AND ABOVE RIGHT: *Vervet monkeys grooming each other in the early morning light.*

Mabula is up to his tricks again this morning. He is becoming increasingly in musth and is more aggressively protecting his herd. I am really worried that he will do something that harms a human and put himself in jeopardy.

OPPOSITE PAGE, ABOVE AND BELOW: *The juggernaut that is Mabula. His tenacity is as impressive as his size.*

Cameron is trying his hardest to give him enough space, but it is a tricky balancing act between the guests who come specifically to see the elephants and Mabula's increasing need to not have anybody intrude.

Today Cameron has managed to have the truck pointing forward as Mabula comes after us. We zoom away fast over the bumpy rough road and Mabula runs just as fast. It is obvious that he still has not hit his full speed.

After a long chase, he breaks off and we think we have outpaced him. Cameron slows down, and we go back to enjoying the scenery. All of a sudden, Mabula pops out of the bush just behind us. He has taken a short cut across a gully, trying to cut us off, I guess. He had to have been moving fast to get where he is, but we heard nothing. Who would have thought that an elephant could sneak up on a person? Luckily we are still in front, so off we zoom again.

We keep thinking he's given up when he comes around a curve and keeps right on coming at us. It takes a while, but we do finally get far enough away for him to lose interest.

ABOVE: *Mabula watches us drive off.*
BELOW: *Surprise! Mabula continues the chase.*

Above: *A gnu out in the open. They are common in the area, but this is our first unobstructed view.*

Left: *At long last, agnother gnu. Our happiness is complete.*

Below: *A poacher's snare draws blood.*

The drive is almost over when we spot some zebras, one of whom keeps shaking her head and rubbing up against any herd member who will stand still for it. The Belgium woman, using binoculars, spots the poacher's snare around the zebra's neck. It is barbed where the noose has been tied, and the thin wire is digging into her neck. She is bleeding. Cameron calls Promise, the head ranger, to report the find and give the general location and direction of the heard. He tells us it is already too hot to take care of it today. The combination of being wounded, sedated and the heat would be too much stress. Tomorrow in the cool early morning, they plan to dart the animal and remove the snare. Assuming, of course, that they can find her.

Left: *A newborn zebra foal. Cameron estimates he's about 2 hours old. His legs look like they were designed by M.C. Escher.*

Below: *Nyala drinking at one of the water holes.*

On our way back to the lodge, we pass three Thula Thula men walking along the side of the road armed with rifles. We hear later that they caught two poachers who were carrying a rifle and an axe. The poachers are now in jail and likely to be there for a long time. Someone asks Cameron if the rangers use force to capture poachers and he says it depends. If the poacher is cooperative, they just arrest him and throw him in jail, but the rangers are prepared to answer aggression with aggression.

Today, in the 104° heat, we do our picnic lunch in the bush. (It was offered as part of our package deal—we would have never thought of it ourselves.) Victor and Cameron tote all the food and gear out to a beautiful clearing under the trees. Victor stays at the site to guard the food from monkeys and baboons while Cameron fetches us from the lodge and Dave and Marie from the camp. It is so hot we need blankets on the truck seats to keep from getting burned and it is impossible to find anywhere cool enough to hang on for the bumpy ride. We arrive at the glade to find a beautifully set table complete with tablecloth, silverware, cloth napkins, and champagne glasses. The chairs even match the tablecloth. It looks festive and idyllic but odd, out in the bush in the middle of nowhere. Robert and I stick with our usual nonalcoholic drinks and Dave drinks beer, but Marie gets into the party spirit and drinks the champagne. The food is delicious, a vegetable frittata even better than yesterday's, plus a lemon tart for desert. We enjoy easy conversation though I cannot recall what we talk about.

ABOVE: *Bush picnic.*

ABOVE RIGHT: *Cameron sets the table.*

RIGHT: *(from left to right) Dave, Marie, Victor, Robert, Cameron*

When we stop to pick up Dave and Marie for the evening drive, the rhinos are on the sidewalk at the tent camp, totally undeterred by the amenities of civilization. Marie has to be repeatedly reminded not to go near them. She wants a picture and is hard to convince that it would be better to do it from the truck.

We find the elephants drinking at the dam tonight, with Mabula nowhere to be seen. The elephants are across the water from us, a perfect location for us to watch them. It is quiet and peaceful. We are totally absorbed in the show.

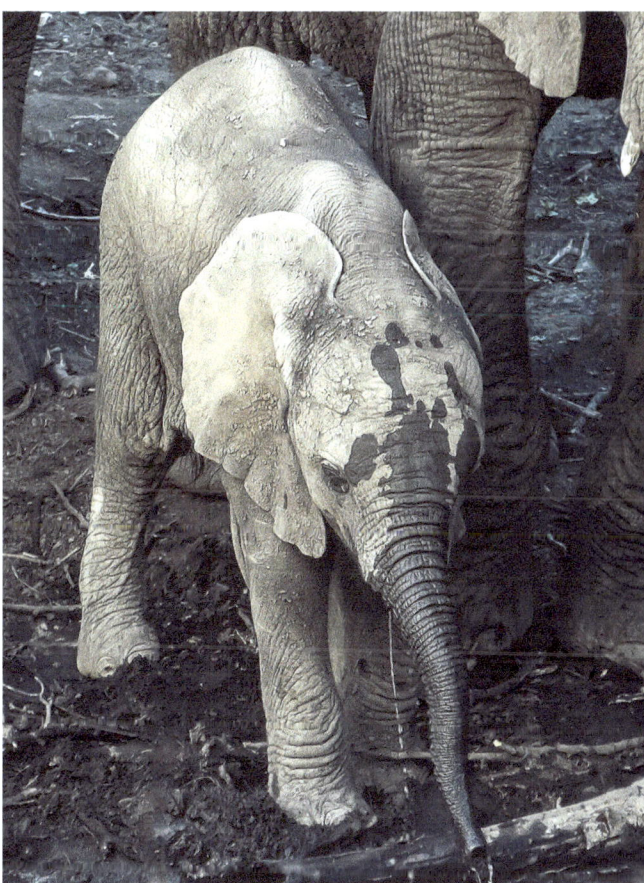

Opposite page top: *Rhinos at the tent camp.*

Opposite page bottom and this page: *Elephants drinking at Gwala Gwala dam. The little one is spotted with water because everybody keeps dripping on her. She doesn't seem to mind.*

Even Cameron is startled when Mabula appears suddenly right in front of the truck. He is once again close enough to touch, but we are all aware that his temper is not nearly as predictable as it was even a few days ago, so we all sit very, very still. There is a certain sense of surrealism in sharing the quiet of the evening with this huge creature. I can see that the secretions staining his cheeks have increased. If he were really threatening us, we'd be overturned and in the water by now. But he isn't. Instead, he paces up and down along the side of the truck looking us over. He is chewing on something and looks just like he is at the movies eating popcorn and we are the entertainment.

Cameron waits patiently for Mabula to get to the back of the truck and then we take off at full speed. It would be easy to get trapped at the dam—Mabula has only to block the one way out. It is much better to avoid putting either us or Mabula in that unhappy situation.

As we are once again zooming down the road, I am tilting and ducking to keep my arms and head away from the sharp thorns of the trees. I remark to Cameron that not only do they offer a bush massage, but they also have bush acupuncture. I am pleased that this makes him laugh.

We are leaving very early in the morning, so we say all our goodbyes at dinner. Mabona, the manager of the lodge, says she will miss Robert because it is so nice to have someone around who just fixes things. I show a quick slide show on my laptop to Cameron and Victor, as they want to see pictures of the cheetah and leopard and I want their help identifying birds. It is hard to say goodbye. We've been here long enough for people to feel like family and I will miss them. I will miss the elephants, too.

Opposite page top: *Mabula at the front of the truck.*

Opposite page bottom: *Yeah, we are that amusing.*

This page top: *Mabula tries again to use a shortcut to follow us, but we are moving fast and he evidently decides we aren't worth trying to catch.*

This page right: *Lolo hides under her mom.*

Next page: *A farewell sunset.*

Afterword

The trip home was even longer and more arduous than the one out. Starting from Durban added an extra leg to the flight plus we had to stop in Rome to refuel. I got help from Ethiopian Airways dealing with the airport in Addis Abba, which made that segment a little easier. Between Addis Abba and Rome, I worked on photos. Robert and I would be parting company in Washington D.C. as he was continuing on for his semi-annual visit to friends and family on the east coast and I was heading home. He wanted pictures to take with him to show off. It was awkward trying to work on the computer in the squished space of economy class. I managed to finish up the slide show and to stay awake during the approach to Rome, figuring this might be the closest I'd ever get to Italy. The lights of Rome were beautiful and I was able to observe that the city was not laid out on a grid. Then I fell asleep and actually slept through the takeoff. I must have been tired.

However nice it was to be back on US soil, Dulles was a nightmare. We walked what seemed like miles to get through passport control, customs and security, only to be misdirected to my connecting gate. We walked miles and miles more, asking directions every so often and seeing no hope of ever getting where we needed to be. I was shaking and sweating from hunger and exhaustion and must have looked like I wasn't doing well because a young woman with a push chair (not really a wheelchair, but the same idea) insisted on helping us. I demurred (do not ask me why) but she was persistent and I'm so glad she was. I'm pretty sure I would have never made it to the gate without her. It was a gross oversight on my part to not ask for help from the airline and I won't make that mistake again.

It took a total of 43 hours to get home and I was a zombie by the time Brook picked me up in Rohnert Park. In fact, I fell asleep on the airport shuttle from San Francisco and almost fell out of my seat. That was a little embarrassing. Brook, bless her heart, had a gallon of milk and my dog, and took me straight home. It took at least a week to get un-jetlagged and used to being home.

I got an emailed newsletter from Thula Thula. Shortly after we left, they started an elephant contraception program with their four adult bull elephants. Mabula is no longer in musth and has stopped chasing the trucks. They have injected the horns of both rhinos with a poisonous substance which is brightly colored, shows up on x-rays, makes people very sick when ingested, and renders the horns completely unusable for poachers. They have posted the property with this information and are advertising the fact far and wide. Both the contraception and horn injections are innovative animal management techniques and the results will be closely followed by other reserves and conservation groups.

Robert got home from his back east trip all in one piece and we are enjoying just being home. I am still amazed, thankful and even a bit proud of us that we had this wonderful adventure. Now, of course, the question is: what next? Okay, not quite ready for the next adventure. Yet.

Above: *A Thula Thula elephant njoying a snack.*

Back Cover: *Frankie near the entrance to Thula Thula.*